This BIG Heart belongs to

_____

OUR SUPERHERO
EDHI
BABA
by WHY Books

This Monday morning every student was ready to present their favourite superhero with the best super power they could find. The teacher was so happy to see the enthusiasm in every child. She organised the jumping students and started the presentations...

Little Edhi saw his mother giving to the needy.

She thought he wouldn't care,

His heart grew bigger everyday a little bit until he became a superhero with a **heart very BIG**

Edhi Baba was the kindest man.
We follow what was his plan.

Notes for parents/teachers

Late Abdul Sattar Edhi had a habit of charity since early childhood, his mother made him donate an amount of money from his daily allowance to the needy. This habit flourished and made Edhi a world renowned humanitarian from Pakistan.

Superheroes have big hearts. Sharing makes your heart big. Sharing with a person in need makes it even bigger. Sharing with a person you do not like or you do not agree with makes your heart the biggest. Help, Share and Donate to be a superhero.

There is an ambulance service by Edhi Foundation which has a network of ambulances all over Pakistan. It facilitates patients in need to reach their destinations. Read more about other ways of donating to and services provided by the Edhi Foundation on official website: https://edhi.org

Whenever there was a natural calamity like flood, earthquake etc. Edhi Sahab used to help either by going there in person or by raising donation for them. Make the kids understand that being kind is the most wonderful super power by giving them examples of local heroes from everyday life. Tell them they do not have to be a millionaire to donate, I donate a portion of what I have, whether it is money or a skill.

DONATE
Let's grow our hearts together!

Printed in Great Britain
by Amazon